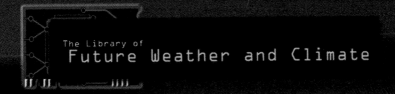

The Library of
Future Weather and Climate

Global Warming
A Threat to Our Future

Paul Stein

The Rosen Publishing Group, Inc.
New York

For Mom and Dad, who have encouraged me in all things

Published in 2001 by The Rosen Publishing Group, Inc.
29 East 21st Street, New York, NY 10010

First Edition

Library of Congress Cataloging-in-Publication Data

Stein, Paul, 1968–
Global warming: a threat to our future / by Paul Stein.—1st ed.
p. cm. — (The library of future weather and climate)
Includes bibliographical references and index.
ISBN 0-8239-3414-4 (lib. bdg.)
1. Global warming—Juvenile literature. [1. Global warming. 2. Climatic changes.] I. Title.
QC981.8.G56 .S74 2000
363.738'74—dc21

00-010385

All temperatures in this book are in degrees Fahrenheit, except where specifically noted. To convert to degrees Celsius, or centigrade, use the following formula:

Celsius temperature = (5 ÷ 9) x (the temperature in Fahrenheit - 32)

Manufactured in the United States of America

Contents

Introduction

Summer 1988. The Mississippi River, the greatest river in North America, evaporates into dry, sandbar-ridden shallows as drought withers the central United States. Five years later, in 1993, the same river swells into a dike-breaking, town-engulfing torrent, submerging over 17 million acres of land and resulting in over $20 billion in damage.

In Chicago, in July 1995, over a period of five days, temperatures as high as 106°F combine with oppressive humidity to cause the deaths of over 400 people. Most severely affected are the elderly, whose bodies are less able to cope with the extreme heat. It's the greatest weather-related disaster in Chicago history, "in several respects totally unprecedented," according to an official study.

During 1982 and 1983, El Niño, a warming of ocean waters in the tropical eastern Pacific, first becomes a household name as it disrupts weather patterns in the Americas. El Niño returns again in the early 1990s, becoming the longest such event on record. And then again, from 1997 to 1998, yet another El Niño event develops, this one in many ways topping that of 1982–1983. In Indonesia, fires

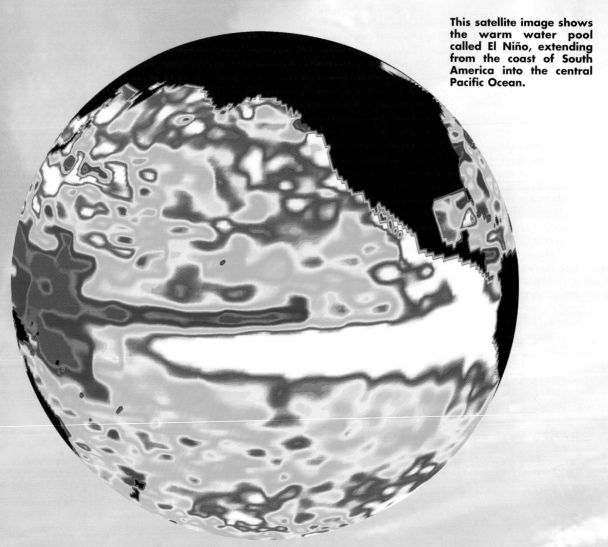

This satellite image shows the warm water pool called El Niño, extending from the coast of South America into the central Pacific Ocean.

scorch the normally rain-soaked tropical forests, sending a cloud of smoke and haze across millions of square miles. El Niño–driven floods and storms wrack parts of South America and the southern United States. There are outbreaks of killer tornadoes in Alabama, Georgia, and—most unusual—Florida, far from the normal "tornado alley" of the Great Plains.

In December 1999, long after El Niño wanes, an astonishing series of windstorms blast western Europe. Packing gusts in excess of 100 mph, these unprecedented tempests flatten forests, blow roofs off buildings, and kill more than 100 people. In France, trees that had weathered storms since the time of Napoleon fall victim by the hundreds.

And all the while, in widely separated corners of the world, many glaciers are in full retreat. From Mt. Kenya in Africa, to the Qori Kalis Glacier in the Andes Mountains in Peru, to the Colombia Glacier in Prince William Sound, Alaska, the ice is shrinking. And at the bottom of the world, large expanses of Antarctic ice known as the Larsen and Wilkins ice shelves begin to crumble away, shrinking in one year nearly half as much as in the previous fifty.

Is the world's weather changing? Like doctors monitoring a feverish patient, year after year meteorologists monitor the mean annual temperature of the earth. But instead of taking the earth's temperature with one thermometer, scientists use almost two thousand, monitored twenty-four hours a day by weather observers all around the world. They track not only air temperatures but also

By analyzing air bubbles in ice cores from Greenland and Antarctica, and reconstructing global temperature trends, climatologists estimate that the 1990s were the warmest decade in 1,000 years.

ocean water temperatures recorded from ships. These air and water temperatures provide an indispensable record of average global temperature over time.

By the end of the twentieth century, there was no doubt: The earth was warming. The year 1999 was the twenty-first consecutive year in which the global mean temperature was above the long-term average. The ten warmest years in recorded history, dating back nearly a century and a half, have all occurred since the early 1980s. The 1990s were the warmest decade in recorded history, with 1998—an El Niño year—being the warmest year. And by analyzing trapped air bubbles in ice cores from Greenland and Antarctica, and reconstructing global temperature trends over the last 1,000 years, climatologists were able to state that in all likelihood the 1990s were the warmest years of the millennium.

Melting glaciers. Record-setting temperatures. More and bigger El Niño events. Vicious storms. Is this the beginning of a long-term and potentially destructive trend in global climate, or is it merely a temporary, natural fluctuation? The answer to this question is rather important to all of us.

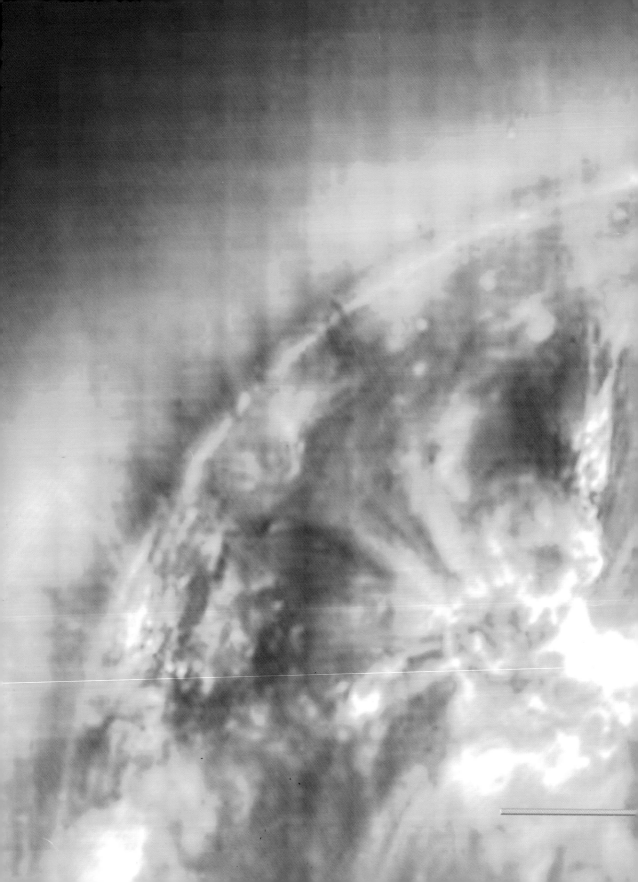

1 The Weather Machine

Scientists looking for answers to the climate puzzle examine the natural processes that control the earth's temperature. Of primary importance among these processes is a kind of energy that travels in the form of invisible electromagnetic waves. This energy, called radiation, has long been known to control the earth's weather machine.

We are awash in radiation, but we are blind to most of it. Different kinds of radiation are distinguished from one another by their wavelength, which is simply the distance from one crest of a wave to the next. Unlike waves of water, however, radiation needs no medium, or substance, through which to pass. Radiation from the Sun, for example, travels 93 million miles through the void of space before striking the earth.

Visible radiation is broken down into different colors of the spectrum, depending on wavelength.

Most people have heard about the dangers of radiation associated with nuclear weapons or nuclear power plants. But radiation takes many forms. Radiation we can see is called light. Color, such as the red of a rose or the blue of the sky, depends on the wavelength of light that reaches our eyes. Shorter wavelengths, on the order of 400 billionths of a meter, appear as purple or blue. Longer wavelengths, around 700 billionths of a meter, appear as red. Beyond these narrow limits, radiation is invisible to us. Though we cannot see them, other kinds of radiation pulse and ripple at the speed of light through the space all around us, and even through us. Ultraviolet radiation from the Sun can burn our eyes and cause skin cancer. Infrared radiation plays a central role in the regulation of global temperature. We can't see infrared radiation, but we can feel it on our skin as the sensation of heat.

Where does radiation come from? Radiation is emitted by the superfast motions of tiny charged particles such as electrons. Every atom of every molecule in everything that exists contains these tiny particles, jostling and whirling at the speed of light. As these charged particles vibrate to and fro, they create waves of electromagnetic energy. The process is not unlike the waves of water generated by a wriggling bug unfortunate enough to land in a pond.

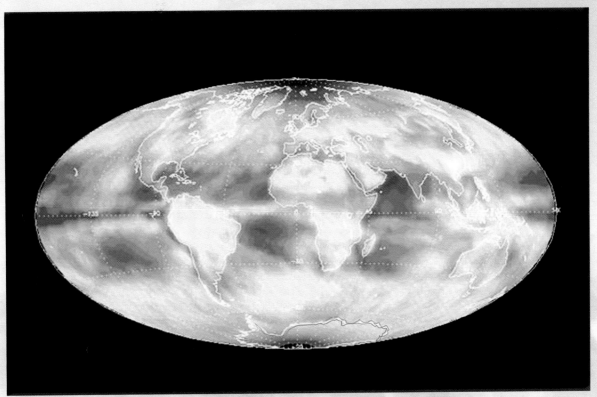

NASA's Clouds and the Earth's Radiant Energy System, or CERES, sensors show the balance between incoming radiation from the Sun and outgoing radiation from the earth.

Since all objects are made up of millions of these energized particles, all objects emit radiation. This book, your body, the earth, and the atmosphere, are all continuously giving off radiation. Not only does everything send out radiation, but everything absorbs radiation. Incoming and outgoing radiation contribute to the total energy, and hence the temperature, of an object. If the object gives off more radiation than it receives, it cools. If an object absorbs more radiation than it gives off, it warms.

The temperature of the surface of the earth, for example, depends on a balance of incoming radiation from the Sun, called solar radiation or insolation, and outgoing radiation from the surface of the earth, called terrestrial radiation. During the day, the earth absorbs

Southern California's dynamic topography plays a critical role in the state's climate.

energy from the Sun's rays. The amount of this incoming solar radiation exceeds the amount of outgoing terrestrial radiation, causing the ground to warm. The atmosphere also warms, not by absorbing radiation from the Sun (most of which passes through air molecules) but mainly by virtue of being in contact with the warm ground.

As night falls, the ground loses its solar heating source. Outgoing terrestrial radiation exceeds the dwindling incoming solar radiation, and the ground cools. As the ground cools, so does the air in contact with it. Thus the balance between incoming solar radiation and outgoing terrestrial radiation is by and large responsible for the daily swings of temperature we all observe: warmer temperatures during the day, and cooler temperatures during the night.

Not only do incoming and outgoing radiation vary from day to night, but they also vary from the earth's equator to its poles. Since the Sun's rays strike the earth more directly in the tropics, solar radiation delivers more energy to a given area in these regions.

Closer to the poles, the story is different. Solar radiation strikes the earth at an oblique angle, delivering a relatively low amount of energy to a given area. In these colder regions, on average, the amount of outgoing terrestrial radiation exceeds the amount of incoming solar radiation.

The difference in incoming versus outgoing radiation between the tropics and the poles, therefore, sets up a strong contrast in temperatures. Air masses of different temperatures have different pressures and densities. Since air at high pressure will flow toward an area of low pressure, the winds blow as the air moves in an attempt to correct this temperature imbalance. Oceans and land masses also warm and cool at different rates, further altering the way in which temperature is distributed across the globe. Add the spin of the earth, and you wind up with thousand-mile-wide masses of air spreading north and south, mixing and clashing along atmospheric boundaries called fronts.

But this is only part of the picture. What has been left out is the continuous transfer of radiation from the ground to the atmosphere, and from the atmosphere to the ground. This exchange of radiation is the source of the famed greenhouse effect. It's a natural process, without which life as we know it could not exist on Earth.

2 The Greenhouse Effect

We have seen that incoming solar radiation warms the ground, which in turn warms the air in contact with it. Certain gases in the atmosphere, known as the greenhouse gases, are much more efficient at absorbing this radiation than other gases. Carbon dioxide (CO_2) is one such greenhouse gas. Others include water vapor, methane, nitrous oxide, chlorofluorocarbons (CFCs), and ozone.

The earth also grows warmer by continuously absorbing radiation emitted by the atmosphere. Air molecules, like all objects, constantly emit radiation. Some of this radiation travels up into space; some down toward the earth. And the amount of atmospheric radiation absorbed by the earth is by no means trivial. In fact, the

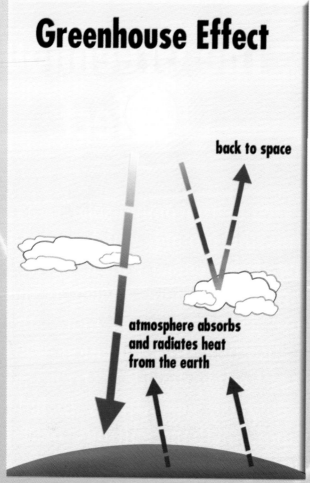

Greenhouse Effect

back to space

atmosphere absorbs
and radiates heat
from the earth

The greenhouse effect results from the heat exchange between the earth, the atmosphere, and the Sun.

earth receives nearly twice as much radiation from the atmosphere as it does directly from the Sun. How can this be?

While the Sun is a strong source of radiation, it appears as a miniature, bright spot in the sky, and only for part of the day. The atmosphere, on the other hand, is a much weaker source of radiation but covers the entire sky day and night. The earth absorbs a significant amount of radiation from the atmosphere.

If the atmosphere did not exist, the earth would absorb energy only from the Sun, and the planet would be much colder than it is now. With only this one source of energy, powerful though the Sun may be, the earth's temperature would be well below freezing. Our planet would be icy and desolate, with a climate similar to Mars in many respects, and devoid of life. But a layer of air molecules hundreds of miles thick surrounds the earth, and these air molecules constantly emit radiation toward the land and water below. The earth therefore receives radiation from two sources: the Sun and the atmosphere. With these two sources of energy, the earth's average temperature is a hospitable 59°F.

The greenhouse effect, therefore, is the warming effect the atmosphere has on our planet. It arises from the constant, invisible exchange of radiation up and down between the air and the earth. If the atmosphere and the ground are continuously adding energy to one another, how does the planet ever stop heating up? This ovenlike scenario actually occurs—but not on Earth. Our nearest planetary neighbor in the direction of the Sun, Venus, is an example of this "runaway" greenhouse effect.

Being close to the Sun, Venus receives twice the amount of solar radiation that the earth does. Most of this energy is reflected back into space by dense clouds of sulfuric acid that shroud the Venusian surface. The energy that does reach the surface, however, contributes to a greenhouse effect so exaggerated that the average temperature on Venus is an incredible 860°F. The reason that Venus has a runaway greenhouse effect is that the Venusian atmosphere is over 96 percent carbon dioxide.

Carbon dioxide attracts the attention of scientists because it is an especially efficient absorber of outgoing terrestrial radiation. It therefore plays an important role in the greenhouse effect. Any changes in the amount of carbon dioxide in our atmosphere may have significant implications for our future climate.

3 Carbon Dioxide in the Atmosphere

On the top of Mauna Loa on the big island of Hawaii, the rocky, barren landscape lies in stark contrast to the lush, warm, tropical paradise that rings the mountain thousands of feet below. So cold is this tropical volcano that snowstorms occasionally lash the peak during winter. Moist winds sweeping in from the Pacific Ocean rise up the 11,000-foot lava slope, forming clouds that can shroud the mountain for days at a time. Scientists have become known for seeking out the harsher corners of the world to gather valuable measurements, and the bleak, windswept summit of Mauna Loa is no exception. Stationed at an observatory near the top of the mountain, atmospheric scientists have been measuring carbon dioxide levels in the air for over four decades.

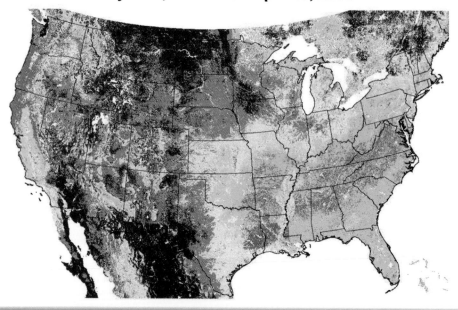

United States
MODIS Land Gross Primary Production
16 day total, March 26 - April 10, 2000

NASA uses its new Moderate Resolution Imaging Spectrodiometer (MODIS) to track the collective photosynthesis of plants almost daily, essentially measuring how the planet is "breathing."

The atmospheric concentration of CO_2 as measured at Mauna Loa has shown an ominous upward trend. In 1959, the first year of measurements, scientists recorded a concentration of 315 parts per million, or ppm for short. In other words, out of every million air molecules, an average of 315 were molecules of carbon dioxide. From 315 ppm in 1959, the concentration of carbon dioxide rose above 320 ppm in the 1960s, over 330 ppm in the 1970s, past 340 ppm in the 1980s, and up to 360 ppm at the turn of the century. And it's still rising. What controls the amount of airborne carbon dioxide? And why has it been steadily increasing?

One natural process that regulates the amount of CO_2 in the atmosphere occurs with the changing of the seasons. From spring through summer and into early autumn, plants and trees take in CO_2 through their leaves and convert it into energy through the process of photosynthesis. As this happens, the concentration of CO_2 in the air decreases. When plants die and trees shed their leaves for the winter months, the carbon stored in the plants is released back into the atmosphere and carbon dioxide levels increase again. This yearly rise and fall of CO_2 levels is like the breathing of the planet.

Some natural processes work over longer periods of time. Rain washes carbon dioxide from the air and erodes calcium from rocks. The calcium and carbon molecules run off into the ocean, where tiny organisms use them to build shells. When the organisms die, the carbon in the shells drifts to the ocean floor. There, the natural movement of the earth's crust carries some of this debris underneath the continents. Compressed under miles of rock, the pressurized carbon becomes gaseous carbon dioxide, which spews back into the atmosphere through volcanoes. The entire process takes about 500,000 years.

Neither one of these natural processes works in a way that might account for the steady rise in CO_2 recorded on Mauna Loa. To determine exactly why carbon dioxide levels are increasing, scientists must look back in time.

In both Antarctica and Greenland, scientists have drilled deep into the ice in order to reconstruct a historical record of the amount of CO_2 in the earth's atmosphere. As layers of snow fall year after year, each layer is compacted under the previous one, eventually hardening into ice. Trapped within the ice are air bubbles, tiny records of the

Burning fossil fuels over the last century has steadily increased the amount of CO_2 in the atmosphere.

gaseous composition of the atmosphere at the time a particular layer formed. Scientists drill into the ice to extract long tubular samples, called ice cores. They examine the trapped bubbles in the ice cores to see how much CO_2 they contain. The deeper into the ice they drill, the further back in time they can look.

Using the ice core data, scientists have been able to determine that the steadily increasing trend in atmospheric CO_2 now being recorded on Mauna Loa actually began around the time of the Industrial Revolution. During that era, from the late eighteenth century to the early nineteenth century, the energy potential of coal was discovered and exploited to drive machines and fuel factories. Coal was dug from the ground and burned in increasing amounts, first in England and other parts of western Europe, then in the United States. In the twentieth century, oil was discovered, and then natural gas. Use of these fossil fuels spread around the world, driving industry and leading to the modern society we know today. Cars, planes, home appliances, and many other modern comforts we take for granted run, either directly or indirectly, on fossil fuels.

So how do fossil fuels relate to the increase in carbon dioxide? Fossil fuels are so named because they are created from the ancient remains of plants and animals compressed deep underground. Plants, like all organic matter, are made from carbon. Over millions of years of pressure far below the surface of the earth, the carbon inside these fossilized plants is transformed into natural gas, oil, and coal. By extracting these fossil fuels from the ground and burning them for energy, we release carbon dioxide into the atmosphere.

The record from the ice cores is clear. Before the Industrial Revolution, the concentration of atmospheric CO_2 was fairly stable at around 280 ppm. Since the Industrial Revolution, as humans have pumped more and more carbon dioxide into the atmosphere through the burning of fossil fuels, the level of CO_2 has increased 30 percent. And according to the yearly tally at Mauna Loa, the trend shows no sign of stopping. In fact, ice cores can give us information about CO_2 levels much further back in history than the eighteenth and nineteenth centuries. Scientists now think that the current amount of CO_2 in the atmosphere is the highest in the last 420,000 years.

We've seen that carbon dioxide plays an important role in the greenhouse effect by efficiently absorbing outgoing terrestrial radiation. Increase the carbon dioxide concentrations, and you increase the greenhouse effect. So, is the global warming scientists have observed over the last twenty years tied to the increasing amounts of carbon dioxide in the atmosphere? The question isn't as easy to answer as it appears.

4 Interpreting the Data

The earth's atmosphere grows warmer or colder, sometimes quickly, sometimes gradually, as a result of many interacting forces. One of the main problems facing climatologists today is trying to determine the cause of the recent global warming. Is it due to carbon dioxide and the greenhouse effect, or is it the result of some other natural warming process?

We're familiar with some of the natural causes of temperature swings: The relative warmth we experience during the day when the Sun is overhead is followed by lower temperatures at night after the Sun has set. A heat wave in the summer may last for several days, broken by rainstorms and followed by cooler air. A cold snap in winter may bring snow and icy winds.

Volcanic activity can cause global temperature changes and variations.

These variations in temperature are caused by the Sun's radiation and the position and tilt of the earth in its orbit at different times of the year.

But the earth's average temperature also naturally changes over much longer time periods, anywhere from decades to centuries or more. For example, the average temperature of the earth can rise or fall following a change in the temperature of the oceans. El Niño, a warming of sea water in the eastern tropical Pacific, is an example of this. Typically, the average temperature of the earth increases slightly during an El Niño event. The year 1998, the warmest on record in the twentieth century, was an El Niño year. Likewise, average global temperatures can cool slightly during a La Niña event, as ocean water temperatures decrease.

Another cause of global temperature change is volcanic activity. Occasionally, large eruptions can spew gases high into the atmosphere. These gases then combine with water vapor to form an atmospheric haze that can block incoming solar radiation. Upper level winds blow this haze around the world, producing a slight planetary cooling. The effect of volcanic haze was recently observed following the eruption in 1991 of Mt. Pinatubo in the Philippines, which blasted 20 million metric tons of sulfur dioxide into the atmosphere. As a result, the average global temperature decreased by up to 1°F for the following two years.

Events that influence the temperature of the earth may also originate far outside the boundaries of our atmosphere. For example, the Sun's energy output changes from a minimum to a maximum level over a period of eleven years. The way in which this variation in energy affects weather patterns on Earth is not fully understood, but scientists think that periods of minimum solar energy output can correspond to periods of colder weather on Earth.

Another factor that can influence climate over even longer time periods is the way in which the earth orbits the Sun. The path the earth takes around the Sun varies slightly over a period of 100,000 years. Also, the angle at which the earth tilts on its axis varies over a period of 41,000 years. Finally, the direction in which the earth is tilted from its orbital plane changes gradually over 19,000 to 23,000 years. These nearly imperceptible changes affect the amount of solar radiation received by the earth and the way in which this radiation is distributed between the equator and the poles. Scientists have attempted to link some of these orbital cycles with the comings and goings of ice ages over the millennia.

The average temperature of the earth, therefore, depends on a variety of natural processes. And all of these processes are

Urban areas naturally absorb heat and become warmer than the surrounding country, an effect called an urban heat island.

occurring at the same time. The earth's tilt changes at the same time that its orbit changes. El Niños and La Niñas come and go, while at the same time the Sun's energy output cycles up and down. Every once in a while, a volcano blows its top and sends a cloud of haze around the globe. And all this is overlaid on the natural daily and seasonal swings of temperature. The sum of these natural cooling and warming processes determines the average temperature of the planet. Warming effects may cancel out cooling effects, or vice versa. Or two events that naturally cause warming may coincide, leading to a period of enhanced global warming.

Most scientists agree that the global warming observed in recent years is at least partially due to the effects of greenhouse gases like carbon dioxide. The presence of so many other natural processes, however, makes it difficult to tell. Some scientists remain skeptical. They point to a couple of potential problems with the observed temperature record.

One way in which the record of observed temperatures may show a warming trend that isn't actually occurring is if the environment around recording sites changes over time. Over the last fifty years or so, cities have grown at a rapid pace. What once was farmland around the edge of many cities has been transformed into miles of new homes. Urban areas, with their asphalt and concrete, naturally absorb heat and become warmer than the surrounding country. In big cities such as Washington, DC, it's not uncommon for outlying areas to be 10 to 20 degrees colder at night compared with the center of the city. This warming effect is due to the presence of what is called an urban heat island.

Temperature records near cities, therefore, may show a warming trend through the years as the city grows and the urban heat island expands. Some speculate that the observed temperature rise in the latter half of the twentieth century is partly, or wholly, due to this kind of artificial urban warming. But research has shown that the warming trend has been recorded not just around cities but also at thermometers stationed in rural areas far from urban sprawl.

Another source of dispute about recent temperature trends comes not from ground-based thermometers but from satellites in orbit thousands of miles above the surface of the earth. Since 1979, satellites have been measuring the temperature of the lower portion of the earth's atmosphere. Whereas thermometers record temperature only several feet above the ground, satellites probe the lowest seven to ten miles of atmosphere. Some analyses of this data show no change in atmospheric temperature, some only a slight warming. The data stands in contrast to the significant warming trend recorded by ground-based observations through the same time period. Scientists expect that the warming rates of air near the ground may be different than higher in the atmosphere, though the difference between the data from surface thermometers and that from satellites remains to be thoroughly explained.

Are we misinterpreting the data? Most scientists don't think so. Is the recently observed global warming just part of the natural evolution of the atmosphere? If so, then perhaps we may expect the climate to swing back to cooler levels in the near future, and we can breathe easier. But if the warming that scientists have recently observed is caused by increasing greenhouse gas levels caused by the burning of fossil fuels, then we may be faced with major problems in the years ahead. Especially as we continue to pump increasing amounts of CO_2 into the atmosphere year after year.

5 Life in a Warmer World

The average global temperature at the end of the twentieth century was about 1°F higher than at the beginning of the century. While one degree seems trivial, it is significant considering that the planet has only warmed by 5 to 9°F since the last ice age, 18,000 to 20,000 years ago. What's more, the rate of temperature rise is accelerating.

Each year, we inject seven billion metric tons of carbon dioxide into the atmosphere. At the current rate of increase, carbon dioxide levels will double before the end of the twenty-first century. Scientists predict that because of this increase in carbon dioxide, the average temperature of the earth will rise anywhere from 2 to 6°F, with a best guess of 3.5°F. Some think this will result in the fastest rate of climate change in the last 10,000 years. What might we expect?

One consequence of global warming will be an increased threat of flooding.

One of the most threatening side effects of a warming atmosphere will be a rise in the level of the oceans. Sea water levels can increase for two reasons. One reason is that as water becomes warmer, individual molecules move around faster, spread farther apart, and occupy more space. This process is known as thermal expansion. Ocean levels can also rise as a result of the inflow of water from melting glaciers and polar ice sheets. Over the last 100 years, the 1°F rise in average global temperature has resulted in a four- to ten-inch rise in ocean levels around the world. By 2100, the best estimate is for an additional sea level rise of twenty inches, though predictions vary from six inches to over three feet.

The effects of such a surge in ocean levels would be tremendous. Nearly 50 percent of the world's population live in coastal zones. Higher water levels would threaten coastal cities such as New York, Venice, and Hong Kong. Coastal storms will become even more destructive as wind and waves drive water farther inland than ever before. If the more extreme predictions come true, some island nations, such as those scattered through the Pacific Ocean, may be submerged completely.

Global warming may also cause an increased threat of floods and droughts. These events may become more frequent as evaporation rates increase in a warmer world. Evaporation is the process whereby liquid water molecules change into invisible, gaseous water vapor. The higher the air temperature, the more quickly water evaporates and the faster the ground dries out. Drought may therefore start earlier and last longer in a warmer climate. Certain parts of the world, known as semiarid regions, will be most vulnerable to drought as evaporation rates increase. The Great Plains of the United States is one such region.

Oddly enough, increased evaporation rates in a warmer climate may lead to more intense rainstorms. Rain occurs as molecules of water vapor in the air stick together and form raindrops. In a warmer atmosphere with higher evaporation rates, it becomes more difficult for water vapor molecules to do this. More water vapor gathers in the air. When a weather system does finally trigger a rainstorm, the extra water vapor in the atmosphere may lead to more intense rainfall and flooding.

Global warming may pose a threat to plant and animal life. Over the centuries, different kinds of plants and animals have adapted to certain levels of rainfall and temperature. A community of plants and animals living in a common natural environment is called a biome. Examples of biomes include grassland, tropical rain forest, and tundra. If the environment of a biome changes, the members of that ecological community will need to adapt or migrate in order to survive.

With the expected rise in temperature during the twenty-first century, scientists predict that climate zones may shift northward by 100 to 350 miles, and upward in altitude by 500 to 1,800 feet. Biomes may experience a similar shift. This may squeeze out existing plants, such as certain varieties of trees that currently exist only along the slopes of mountain ranges. Climate may also change faster than plants are able to migrate. Some species may become isolated or even extinct.

When it comes to plant life, however, global warming may actually have some benefits. The growing season will last longer in northern lattitudes in a warmed world. Certain kinds of crops may be grown where they have never thrived before. Trees and plants may grow faster and larger because of the "fertilization effect." Trees and plants convert CO_2 and water into plant material using sunlight. The more CO_2 in the air, the more efficient this process becomes. The fertilization effect, however, must compete with an increased potential for drought. Not all plants and crops will benefit.

Climate change may affect human health. A warmer climate may cause more frequent heat waves. With more water vapor in the air, humidity levels will be higher. This combination of heat and humidity is oppressive and potentially deadly during summertime.

The threat from disease may also increase on a warmer planet. Warmer temperatures favor the breeding of mosquitoes, which are known to carry diseases such as malaria. Scientists estimate that if some of the higher predicted temperature increases are reached, the percentage of the world population exposed to malaria may increase from the current level of 45 percent to as high as 60 percent.

Perhaps the most disturbing aspect of global warming, however, is its potential for surprise. Evidence from ice cores indicates that the earth's climate has not always changed gradually. It seems as though the climate can operate in different modes, like the different speeds of a bike or the gears of a car. When certain thresholds are reached, the climate may suddenly "shift" into a new mode.

One example of this kind of rapid climatic shift occurred over 12,000 years ago as the earth was freezing under a 1,500-year-long cold spell known as the Younger Dryas event. Suddenly, within a span of just fifty years, a spectacular climate shift occurred. The average global temperature soared over 12°F and precipitation increased by 50 percent. Scientists think that these kinds of sudden and unpredictable climate shifts may be triggered by changes in the ocean's circulation. Global warming can disrupt ocean currents as glacial melting or increased rainfall pours large amounts of freshwater into the salty oceans.

The evidence that the earth's climate is capable of changing rapidly and unexpectedly is startlingly clear. The amount of global warming necessary to trigger such a catastrophic event is unknown.

6 The Uncertain Future

Global warming presents a potentially frightening vision for the future. Rising oceans, more frequent and severe droughts and floods, shifting biomes—how confident are scientists that these events will come to pass? And how do they arrive at such predictions?

There is a significant amount of uncertainty about the future state of the earth's climate. The atmosphere is an extremely complex natural system, and it doesn't act in isolation. The atmosphere, the oceans, the continents, human activities, and plant and animal life all influence one another.

When two or more events affect one another, as often happens with the earth's climate, sometimes they may enhance one

Global warming could have a significant impact on many fragile ecosystems on Earth, such as this rain forest near Sao Paulo, Brazil.

another in a process known as positive feedback, or they may cancel one another out in a process known as negative feedback. These feedback mechanisms in our climate system are sources of uncertainty about the way the atmosphere will behave in a warmer world.

Water vapor, for example, can promote both positive and negative feedback mechanisms. In a warmer world, a positive feedback may occur as evaporation rates increase. Increasing evaporation will lead to greater amounts of water vapor in the air, and water vapor is a greenhouse gas. The more water vapor in the air, the stronger the greenhouse effect becomes and the more the planet warms. The warmer the planet, the more water vapor in the air, which leads to even more warming.

Water vapor may also produce a negative feedback. The higher the concentration of water vapor in the air, the greater amount of clouds in the atmosphere. Clouds reflect incoming solar radiation, causing the planet to become cooler. To complicate the picture, the role that clouds play in the climate puzzle depends on their height and thickness. Thin, high clouds are thought to lead to further warming as they absorb outgoing terrestrial radiation and let incoming solar radiation through. Thick, low clouds, on the other hand, may have a cooling effect as they block sunlight from reaching the earth's surface.

Another positive feedback may arise from the melting of ice and snow near the earth's poles. Ice and snow, owing to their bright white color, reflect solar radiation away from the earth's surface. This results in lower air temperatures. In a warmer world, however, shrinking snow and ice cover near the poles will reflect less sunlight, allowing the earth to become warmer. The warmer the earth, the more snow and ice melt, and the less solar radiation is reflected away from the planet.

Oceans are one of the greatest sources of uncertainty concerning the future state of the climate. Ocean water, for example, absorbs heat much more slowly than land. Some scientists think that the rate at which the atmosphere will warm in coming years will be slowed by the ability of the ocean to store some of the heat building up in the atmosphere.

As we've seen, the warmer the oceans become, the higher they rise and the greater they threaten coastal regions. Also, what of El Niño or La Niña in a warmer world? One possibility is that El Niño, the periodic warming of tropical Pacific waters, may become stronger

Bright white ice and snow reflect solar radiation away from the earth's surface, resulting in lower air temperatures.

and more frequent. As we've seen from El Niño events in the late twentieth century, this may have repercussions for global weather. But most scientists would argue that we still don't know enough about the processes that govern the formation and decay of El Niño events to speculate how El Niño may behave in a warmer atmosphere.

Scientists must consider all these questions, and more, in trying to come to terms with the possible outcomes of a warmer planet. To grapple with these problems they use powerful supercomputers to run extremely complex simulations of the earth's atmosphere and oceans. These simulations are called computer models, and they use advanced mathematical equations to represent the physical laws that control the behavior of air and water.

It's impossible for any computer to calculate the motions and temperatures of every air and water molecule across the planet into the future. Computer models, therefore, must make drastic simplifications about the way the natural world works. These shortcuts permit models to crunch the necessary numbers and complete their predictions in a relatively short period of time. But they also introduce potential errors into the results. Scientists gain confidence in these less-than-perfect models by first using them to simulate historical weather patterns and then comparing the model's predictions with what actually happened. As for future predictions, scientists look for consistency in results. If many different computer models arrive at similar climate predictions, it may mean they're honing in on a realistic scenario.

Over the last twenty years or so, the models have arrived at a common vision for our future climate, assuming a doubling of carbon dioxide amounts in the atmosphere. They all show rising global temperatures, with most warming occurring at night and during the winter as the snow and ice cover shrinks over time. A common model prediction is for a greater frequency of droughts and flooding rains, as evaporation rates increase and more water vapor gets pumped into the air.

Results from computer models are published in professional scientific journals and debated by scientists around the world. There remains much disagreement about the role certain feedback processes may play in the eventual outcome of a warmed planet. Computer models have a particularly difficult time simulating some of the processes that contribute to feedback mechanisms, such as clouds and ocean currents.

As computer models become faster and more precise, scientists may begin to unravel some of these mysteries in the coming years. We hope that the rate at which we gain knowledge will outpace the rate of global warming.

7 The Response

Makers of public policy, such as government officials, need to cut through the scientific debate and extract the essential information that enables them to prepare for the possibility of a changing climate. They need to know what the best scientific guess is, even though it is just a guess. They need information, as unbiased as possible, communicated efficiently and in nontechnical language. In 1988, an international group of scientists convened in Geneva, Switzerland, for this very purpose.

The Intergovernmental Panel on Climate Change, or IPCC, consists of hundreds of scientists working together toward three goals. The first goal is to

The Intergovernmental Panel on Climate Change, or IPCC, is trying to discover how climate changes will impact the planet Earth and its people.

assess the most up-to-date information on climate change. What are recent temperature trends showing? At what rate are greenhouse gases increasing? What kind of evidence for climate change is currently being observed? What's the best guess right now for the magnitude of climate change over the next hundred years?

The second goal of the IPCC is to examine how changes in climate might impact the earth, and human beings in particular. How might these trends continue into the future? How will rising ocean levels affect coastal regions? How might biomes migrate in a warmed world, and what might be the impact on agriculture and water supplies?

The third goal is to suggest the most prudent ways of dealing with a changing climate. Given our best estimation of what might happen, what are the things we can do now to lessen potential problems in the future? How does the efficiency with which we use energy affect the rate at which we emit carbon dioxide into the air, and what can we do to modify our energy use to limit negative impacts on the climate?

When it comes to global warming, the IPCC is the world authority. In its 1995 report, the IPCC stated that "the balance of evidence suggests a discernable human influence on global climate." In other words, greenhouse gas emissions are at least partially responsible for the global warming observed over the last twenty years. The IPCC predicted a 2 to 6°F average global temperature increase over the next century, with a best guess of 3.5°F. While this predicted increase was slightly less than the original 1990 prediction, it still represents a change in the weather unlike any seen in thousands of years.

Since climate change is a global problem, the response must be global as well. During the first two weeks of December 1997, representatives from over 150 countries convened in Kyoto, Japan, to discuss the potential threat from global warming. Recognizing that the main cause of global warming is the burning of fossil fuels and the release of greater amounts of greenhouse gases into the atmosphere, their stated purpose was "to agree on legally binding targets and timetables for reducing greenhouse gas emissions."

Reducing greenhouse gas emissions involves developing new energy sources and making existing energy production more efficient.

When people think of fossil fuels and greenhouse gas emissions, they often think of gas-burning cars or pollution from factory smokestacks. But we're all more responsible for greenhouse gas emissions than we may think. Turn on a light, for example, and you use electricity, which comes from a power plant. Many power plants in the United States today still burn coal to create electricity. By using electricity, we contribute to the emission of carbon dioxide into the atmosphere.

Energy is a worldwide multibillion dollar industry, and reducing greenhouse gas emissions raises troublesome issues. Many people think that the solution to global warming requires a major change in the way we produce and consume energy. In order to stop adding carbon dioxide and other greenhouse gases to the atmosphere, we need to stop relying on coal, gas, and oil. Alternative energy sources, such as solar energy or wind power, are available.

Most of these new energy sources, however, are impractical for the increasing power needs of large nations. Engineers and scientists need to develop and improve the efficiency of these alternative energy sources in order to make them a viable option in the decades ahead. Faced with the prospects of a worldwide decline in the use of fossil fuels, most representatives of the energy industry view cuts in greenhouse gases as a threat to their business.

Who will pay for it all? At Kyoto in 1997, this debate split the participating countries into competing groups. Poorer, developing countries insisted that since the rich nations like the United States had contributed the most to greenhouse gas emissions over the last

The European Union's environment commissioner, Ritt Bjerregaard of Denmark, is surrounded by reporters as she enters the global warming conference in Kyoto, Japan in 1997.

couple of centuries, they should shoulder more of the burden in fixing the problem. Rich countries, in turn, were concerned about any kind of cuts in greenhouse gas emissions that would hurt their economies.

The final outcome of the meeting, a resolution called the Kyoto Protocol, called for the industrialized countries to cut greenhouse gas emissions by an average of 5 percent below 1990 levels for the years 2008 through 2012. But there are various loopholes that allow countries to achieve their goals without reducing emissions. For example, rich countries can get credit for investing in emission-saving projects in poorer nations. Countries can not only decrease

Educate Yourself

1. Decide on the issues for yourself. In order to make sound judgments, you need to be informed. Know the science behind global warming.

2. Know your sources. A responsibility of living in the information age is knowing who is making claims and why. When in doubt, rely on the IPCC as a thorough and authoritative source for data on global warming.

3. Learn about what our elected officials in government think about the problem of global warming. When it comes time to vote, use this knowledge to make informed choices.

4. Think about energy and how we use it. Greenhouse gases don't just come from cars and factories. What can you do to use energy more efficiently, avoid energy waste, and lessen the amount of energy you consume on a daily basis?

5. Learn more about the processes that naturally remove carbon dioxide from the atmosphere. Is there anything you can do to contribute to the natural recycling of carbon dioxide?

their rate of greenhouse gas emission but can increase the rate at which CO_2 is naturally absorbed. One way to do this is to plant more forests, which absorb CO_2 from the air.

In order to become law in the United States, the Kyoto Protocol must be passed by the Senate with a two-thirds majority vote. As of summer 2000, the Clinton administration had not yet submitted the bill for passage. Not enough members of the Senate yet support the protocol, mainly because of the impact it might have on the energy industry and the economy.

Even more discouraging, however, is that even if all participating nations cut greenhouse gas emissions to the levels called for in the Kyoto Protocol, the cuts would only slow the rate of CO_2 increase. They would not stop greenhouse gas emissions. This will do little to avert the potential climate change in the next century.

Conclusion

Climate change is real. Most scientists think that our warming planet is the result of increased greenhouse gas emissions, especially carbon dioxide. As more of these gases gather in the atmosphere, they may pose a serious threat to our climate and our way of life over the next century and beyond. Though some consequences of global warming may be beneficial, such as the CO_2 "fertilization effect" on crops, many more have the capability to inflict serious damage and disruption on the nations of the world. Governments are responding to this threat, but slowly. In the meantime, is there anything you can do to help?

Glossary

biome A community of plants and animals living in a common natural environment. Examples of biomes include rain forest, desert, and tundra.

climate The average weather conditions of a region over a long period of time, generally decades or more.

climatologist A scientist who studies the climate.

computer model A computer program that simulates the atmosphere and oceans and how they change over time. These models predict how the climate might change as a result of increasing greenhouse gases in the atmosphere.

El Niño A warming of ocean water in the tropical eastern Pacific. When El Niño becomes particularly strong, it can affect weather patterns worldwide.

evaporation The process whereby liquid water changes into invisible, gaseous water vapor.

feedback The phenomenon in which two processes or events influence one another. Feedback can be negative, where the two processes act to cancel one another out, or positive, where the processes act to enhance one another.

fertilization effect The process by which increasing amounts of carbon dioxide in the atmosphere enhance the natural processes that cause plants to grow.

fossil fuel Any fuel made from the decayed remains of ancient plant and animal life; includes coal, natural gas, and oil.

greenhouse effect The naturally occurring process whereby the earth is warmer than it otherwise would be because of the presence of the atmosphere.

greenhouse gases Any gases that efficiently absorb outgoing radiation from the earth, thereby contributing to the greenhouse effect. The main greenhouse gases are water vapor, carbon dioxide, methane, nitrous oxide, chlorofluorocarbons (CFCs), and ozone.

ice core An ice sample in the shape of a tube drilled out from ice sheets. Scientists use ice cores to sample trapped air bubbles from hundreds or thousands of years ago.

Industrial Revolution The rapid growth of factories and industry in the eighteenth and nineteenth centuries, supported by the burning of coal for energy. The onset of the Industrial Revolution led to increasing amounts of carbon dioxide in the atmosphere.

IPCC The Intergovernmental Panel on Climate Change. A multinational group of scientists who assess the state of global warming and report to governments and policymakers.

La Niña A cooling of ocean water in the eastern tropical Pacific. Like El Niño, a strong La Niña can influence weather patterns around the world.

photosynthesis   The process whereby plants use sunlight to convert carbon dioxide and water into plant tissues.

radiation   Energy in the form of invisible electromagnetic waves that travel at the speed of light.

runaway greenhouse effect   An exaggerated greenhouse effect, caused when the atmosphere contains a high percentage of greenhouse gases at high pressures and densities. The planet Venus has a runaway greenhouse effect.

solar radiation   Radiation emitted by the Sun. Solar radiation consists of about 47 percent infrared radiation, 46 percent visible radiation, and 7 percent ultraviolet radiation.

terrestrial radiation   Radiation emitted by the earth, consisting mostly of wavelengths in the infrared range.

thermal expansion   The process by which water increases in volume because of increasing water temperature.

For More Information

American Meteorological Society (AMS)
45 Beacon Street
Boston, MA 02108-3693
Web site: http://www.ametsoc.org/AMS

Climate Prediction Center (CPC)
World Weather Building
5200 Auth Road, Room 800
Camp Springs, MD 20746
Web site: http://www.nnic.noaa.gov/cpc

Intergovernmental Panel on
        Climate Change (IPCC)
c/o World Meteorological Organization
7 bis Avenue de la Paix, C.P. 2300
CH-1211 Geneva 2
Switzerland
Web site: http://www.ipcc.ch

National Climatic Data Center (NCDC)
Federal Building
151 Patton Avenue
Asheville, NC 28801-5001
Web site: http://www.ncdc.noaa.gov

Weatherwise Magazine
Heldref Publications
1319 18th Street NW
Washington, DC 20036-1802
Web site: http://www.weatherwise.org

In Canada

Environment Canada Inquiry Centre
351 St. Joseph Boulevard
Hull, PQ K1A 0H3
Web site: http://www.ec.gc.ca/prod/inqry-e.html

Web Sites

Due to the changing nature of Internet links, the Rosen Publishing Group, Inc., has developed an online list of Web sites related to the subject of this book. This site is updated regularly. Please use this link to access the list:

http://www.rosenlinks.com/lfw/glwa

For Further Reading

Intergovernmental Panel on Climate Change. *IPCC Second Assessment Report on Climate Change.* Geneva, Switzerland: IPCC, 1995.

Stevens, William K. *The Change in the Weather: People, Weather, and the Science of Climate.* New York: Delacorte Press, 1999.

Watson, Robert T., ed. *The Regional Impacts of Climate Change: An Assessment of Vulnerability.* New York: Cambridge University Press, 1997.

Index

About the Author

Paul Stein has a B.S. in meteorology from Pennsylvania State University. He has eight years' experience as a weather forecaster, most recently as a senior meteorologist for the Weather Channel. Currently, he develops computer systems and software that display and process weather-related data.

Photo Credits

Cover © DigitalVision: sunset.

Cover inset © TOMS science team and the Scientific Visualization Studio, NASA: a large ozone hole over Antarctica.

Front matter and back matter © DigitalVision:

Introduction background: KidSat, NASA JPL: fires at the southern tip of Sumatra, Indonesia.

Chapter 1 background © SOHO Extreme ultraviolet imaging telescope, ESA/NASA: solar flare from outer space.

Chapter 2 background © Pictor: sunset.

Chapter 3 background © George Gerster/Photo Researchers, Inc.: Volcanoes National Park, Hawaii.

Chapter 4 background © DigitalVision: parched landscape.

Chapter 5 background © Artville Weatherstock: ocean waves.

Chapter 6 background © The Image Bank: winter in Krokskogen, Norway.

Chapter 7 background © Telegraph Colour Library/FPG International: solar panels.

P. 6 © TOPEX/Poseidon, NASA JPL; p. 8 © Elements of Nature; pp. 30–31, 44 © Pictor; p. 13 © CERES instrument team; p. 14 © NASA/JPL/NIMA; p. 22 © Steven Running, University of Montana, NTSG; p. 24 © Corbis; p. 28 © DigitalVision; p. 36 Artville Weatherstock; p. 42 © The Image Bank; pp. 48, 51 © AP/Worldwide.

Series Design and Layout

Geri Giordano